Teeny Tiny Tingly Tales

by nancy van laan

illustrated by victoria chess

an anne schwartz book
atheneum books for young readers
New York London Toronto Sydney Singapore

For my teeny tiny grandson—boo!
—N. V. L.

Atheneum Books for Young Readers
An imprint of Simon & Schuster Children's Publishing Division
1230 Avenue of the Americas
New York, New York 10020

Book design by Ann Bobco and Kristin Smith
The text of this book is set in Romic.
The illustrations are rendered in acrylics, watercolor, pastels, colored pencil, and pencil.

Printed in the United States of America

2 4 6 8 10 9 7 5 3 1

Library of Congress Cataloging-in-Publication Data
Van Laan, Nancy.
Teeny tiny tingly tales / by Nancy Van Laan ; illustrated by Victoria Chess. - 1st ed.
p. cm.
"An Anne Schwartz book."
Summary: Three rhyming scary stories.
ISBN 0-689-81875-0
1. Horror tales, American. 2. Children's stories, American.
[1. Horror stories. 2. Short stories. 3. Stories in rhyme.]
I. Chess, Victoria; ill. II. Title.
PZ8.3.V47Tg 1999
[E]—dc21
97-37452

FIRST
EDITION

Old
Doctor
Wango Tango

Old Doctor Wango Tango
had a long, red nose;
a rosy, blowsy, noisy, nosey,
long, red nose.

Dirty Doctor Wango Tango
sometimes wore a vest.
And a tie full of fleas
hung down to his knees,
that is, when he bothered to dress.

Mean Doctor Wango Tango
had a lumpy, lazy cat;
a leapy, creepy, weepy cat
who sleepied in his hat.

Dreadful Doctor Wango Tango
kept a dog that wouldn't grow,
and a wimbly bimbly, lamey tamey,
coal black crow.

Wicked Doctor Wango Tango
called his poor horse Sam.
His dog was Towser, his cat was Mouser,
his crow, Fool Flippety Flam.

Stingy Doctor Wango Tango
gave his animals nothing to eat.
Not a bit nor a bite,
not a crust nor a crumb,
just pebbles and grass as a treat.

Foolish Doctor Wango Tango
went out one day to ride,
with Mouser asleep in the hat
on his head
and Towser and Flam by his side.

Old Doctor Wango Tango

rode to the tip of a hill,

high up where the trees were bare,

and the wahooing wind brought a chill,

as it whirled and it hurled

and it hailed and it wailed

and it shrieked with a screech that was shrill.

A A A A A A A A A H H H H —

WHOOOOOOOOOOO!

Away blew Wango Tango!

Away blew Sam!

Away blew Towser

And mean little Mouser!

Away blew Flippety Flam!

It

Two legs inside a pair of pants
came bounding down the stairs.
They danced a jig
and spun around.

Then something *else*
came whooshing down.

Two arms inside a tattered shirt
came floating down the stairs.
They waved and clapped and flappity flapped.

Then something *else*
came thumping down.

One hairy head, a bouncing head,
came
BUMP
    BUMP
       down
         the
           stairs.

It crossed its eyes,

and grumpity grumped,

and knocked the others down.

Slowly IT stood,
stuck together!
Slowly IT turned
all around.
With a
deafening roar,
IT went *through*
the door.
IT wiggled
and wobbled
and giggled
and gobbled,
then . . .

slowly IT strolled to town.

The Hairy Toe

A little old lady
was picking peas
when she felt a tickle
beneath her knees.

The little old lady said,
"Oh! Oh! Oh!
Why, looky here—
A hairy toe!"

So the little old lady
dug way down
and buried the hairy toe
deep in the ground.

When the little old lady
got back home,
along came the wind
and SOMETHING moaned:

Give me back my hairy toe!

Give me back

The little old lady jumped into bed.

She pulled the covers right over her head.

As the rumbling wind growled under the door,

SOMETHING creeped across the floor.

my hairy toe!

The little old lady
could stand no more.
She jumped out of bed
and ran for the door.

She dug and dug
and dug way down
and pulled that toe
right out of the ground.

Then she tossed it as far
as she could throw
to the SOMETHING that wanted
its hairy toe.

"I hope you're happy now,"
she said.
And the little old lady
went back to bed.